Believers with Benefits

Jubilee Mosley

ISBN: 0-9853-7620-1
ISBN-13: 9780985376208

Dedication

~To the God who was, and is, and is to come~

Acknowledgments

To my beloved husband, Will, I appreciate all of your love and just as equally, your encouragement. You have encouraged me to capture my dreams and to just...GO FOR IT! I love you! To Doris M. Stewart, my grandmother, I still miss you and I thank God that your prayers for me are still being answered even now. Rest in peace in the arms of God. To my father, Micah J. Ransome, who taught me what tithing was all about when I was just a young girl. Thank you for not only being a hearer of the word of God but a doer also. To Pastor Paul B. Mitchell, Senior Pastor of Changing Lives Christian Center, the greatest church in the world! Thank you for your in-depth, clear, and practical teaching on tithing over the years. God has used you to increase my understanding of tithing and offering. My life is all the more blessed because of your obedience to Him.

Contents

Introduction

The issue of tithing is an age-old debate. Should I? Should I not? Some say tithing is an Old Testament requirement under the law that can and should be disregarded because...it's old. People inquire whether they should tithe from the gross or net? Can I give a tithe and no offering or an offering and no tithe? How am I going to pay all of my bills when a large portion of what I make monthly goes to tithes? Living the "good life" and tithing is impossible! What's the difference anyway? Why does God need **my** money? Isn't He All- Sufficient? Hmm...I really could use this money to pay some bills or buy those shoes I've had my eye on for months now. I totally deserve to be happy. I mean...I work so hard and I should look like it. Maybe I'll pay my tithes next month. Next month never comes.

A benefit is "something that promotes or enhances well-being or an advantage." The word benefit also means "a payment made or an entitlement available in accordance with a wage agreement, an insurance policy, or public assistance program." God's promises around provision and enhancing our earthly financial experiences are directly linked to our faithful giving of tithes and offerings. Tithing is specifically linked to 10 percent of income, a portion set aside for God, while offering refers to anything given *above* the tithe or a sacrificial gift connected to a specific need or purpose in your life.

Think of tithing as "GHAP"—God's Heavenly Assistance Program. God's "wage agreement" goes like this: I will give to you in abundance and cause you never to be in lack for as long as you honor Me by giving a portion back to Me. All God requires is 10 percent out of every 100 percent. Not a bad deal, right? Giving pleases God and causes Him to bless us. He wants us to have *more* than enough and wants to ensure that all of our needs—spiritual, physical, relational, and financial—are met. Here's some more proof that God's desire is for us to have more than enough. Proverbs 3:9 says:

Honor the Lord with your possessions

*And with the **first fruits** of **all** your increase; So your barns will be filled with plenty and your vats will overflow with new wine.*

There is also evidence of the tithing principle way before it is mentioned in Malachi. Let's go to Genesis chapter 2, verse 15. It says:

Then the Lord God took the man and put him the Garden of Eden to tend and keep it. And the Lord God commanded the man, saying, "Of every tree of the garden you may freely eat but of the tree of the knowledge of good and evil you shall not eat, for in the day that you eat of it you shall surely die."

This is the first biblical example of a tithe—a portion of God's goodness and provision set aside and set apart for His kingdom. So let's put this into context. God told Adam that he could enjoy ALL the goodness of the Garden of Eden with the exception of *one* tree. The tree is symbolic for the 10 percent we pay in tithes. The remainder of the Garden of Eden is the 90 percent…yes the 90 percent that God blesses and allows us to keep as a result of our obedience to His Word. Now, to be clear, we need God's blessing on our finances. Without God's blessing on our finances, a dollar is just a dollar and a check is just a check. God's blessing on our finances helps to solve financial problems and problems that even wealth cannot solve alone. God doesn't just want us to be saved and sanctified believers—even though being saved and sanctified is a wonderful thing. He wants us to access the "more" He has for us. Just think of the more as "fringe benefits." In human resource management, fringe benefits are defined as any type of "compensation in addition to direct wages or salaries." For the sake of comparison, and not to demean Christ's finished work on Calvary, let's just say that as believers some of our "direct wages" include the gifts of salvation, redemption, and eternal life. When we become believers who sow into God's kingdom by way of our tithes and offerings, we now step into a realm that grants us access to the fringe benefits of God.

In addition to God's basic benefits, tithing grants us access to the realm where the abundant, more-than-enough, harvest-to-harvest, blessed-to-be-a-blessing life resides. God wants us to enjoy our everyday lives and do business on His behalf until He returns. How can we do this if we lack resources? He wants us to be lenders and not borrowers, above and not beneath, the head and not the tail (Deuteronomy 28:12). God wants us to be financially fit so that we can do great things in His name, maintain the blessings He has given us, make a difference in His name, *and* enjoy our lives here on earth. Being a believer with benefits is a wonderful thing. Believers with benefits can help to advance the kingdom of God here on earth and live life in the overflow.

Chapter 1
Why Give to God?

God wants to bless us. God has so many great things stored up for us. God does not **need** our money. He is All-Sufficient. However, in order to carry out the mandate set by God to spread the Gospel all around the globe, which brings salvation, healing, and restoration, the church does need the money. God needs our earthly hands to carry out His Heavenly plan. He has tied the fruition of our need to seed and forever linked us to His purpose of advancing His kingdom on earth, which is the most important mandate of all. Just like there is a worldly mandate to educate children, protect our country, fight crime, keep our streets clean and well paved, provide electricity and clean water, and collect our garbage, there is a spiritual mandate to share Christ's message of salvation, hope, and a future all over the world. No stone must be left unturned when it comes to spreading the Gospel of Jesus Christ. Television media, print media, electricity, food, missions efforts, and the cost to run any ministry, whether it is mega or not, is more than just mere pennies. The Bible exhorts us in Matthew 16:16 to do this work. It says:

Then the eleven disciples went to Galilee, to the mountain where Jesus had told them to go. When they saw him, they worshiped him; but some doubted. Then Jesus came to them and said, "All authority in heaven and on earth has been given to me. Therefore go and make disciples of all nations, baptizing them in the name of the Father and of the Son and of the Holy Spirit, and teaching them to obey everything I have commanded you. And surely I am with you always, to the very end of the age."

Three days after Jesus was crucified, removed from the cross, and buried in a tomb, the Roman soldiers went to look for him and to their great displeasure, found that He was gone.

The soldiers had done everything in their power to annihilate Christ—even down to the very memory of Him. They placed a crown of thorns on His head, pierced Him with nails in His hands and feet, spat on Him repeatedly, beat Him with a whip and cat-of-nine-tails all over his human body until He was unrecognizable, and finally pierced His side to affirm that He was indeed dead. So, how is it now that this man, who was considered the greatest imposter and blasphemer ever to have lived, is no longer where He was laid? How could they explain this to Pilate? The Roman soldiers were left with a great dilemma. They gathered and again plotted against the Savior. Here's how the events following Christ's crucifixion and resurrection are captured in the Bible in Matthew 28:11 (NIV 1984):

The Guards' Report

While the women were on their way, some of the guards went into the city and reported to the chief priests everything *that had happened. When the chief priests had met with the elders and devised a plan, **they gave the soldiers a large sum of money**, telling them, "You are to say, 'His disciples came during the night and stole him away while we were asleep.' If this report gets to the governor, we will satisfy him and keep you out of trouble." So the soldiers took the money and did as they were instructed. And this story has been widely circulated among the Jews to this very day.*

You see, the chief priests and the elders concluded, after they consulted with one another, that bribing the soldiers and inducing them to tell a lie was the only way left. They wanted to convince the world that Jesus, despite all the security measures put into place, had really been stolen away. This would mean that Jesus's prophecy could be called a failure and that He really was not the Messiah and Son of the living God. According to the scriptures, the soldiers were given large sums of money to hide the truth and to share a message they knew was false.

Here we see money being used to spread a message contrary to God's word, which is an evil report. If it takes large sums of money to spread a lie, how much money will it take to spread the truth? How much will it cost to submit to people all over the world that Christ is indeed raised from the dead, that He lives today, and that He cares? How much will it cost to help those in need both here and abroad? Tons of money. Billions of dollars. Mucho dinero. Beaucoup d'argent. God requires believers to return to Him a portion of what He so graciously and freely gave. God is the source of life, not our jobs, our businesses, our children, our spouses, or our prestigious country clubs. If we want God's attention, if we want God to breathe favor, long life, divine acceleration, and consistent access to the "more" that He has for us and the generations that will come after us, then we must be in covenant with Him. We can start honoring God's plan for provision by giving tithes and offerings. Now, don't get me wrong, accepting Jesus Christ as Lord and Savior is definitely the best step anyone could ever take and the only way to receive eternal life. He sets us free from bondage and gives life anew, which is priceless. Because of Christ's finished work on Calvary, we automatically have access to basic benefits such as freedom, everlasting life (John 3:16), and the opportunity to live life free of guilt, condemnation, fear, and shame. When we die, we are assured that we will see Christ and live with Him forever in Paradise (1 Thessalonians 4:15). God has even promised to prosper us, but as my pastor always says, "We have a degree of liability in the matter." If we acknowledge, implement, and consistently live by the kingdom system (God's way of thinking) by sowing cheerfully, we will reap bountifully (2 Corinthians 9:6-8). These are the "fringe benefits" of God. Not every believer will live a life of "all-sufficiency in all things" like Paul stated in 2 Corinthians 9:6-8, because not every believer will take God at His word concerning all things. Some believers will live their lives from paycheck to paycheck and some will work year after year at dead-end jobs. Some will be unable to receive or hold on to opportunities for increase, unable to receive witty ideas from the

Lord, unable to walk into new seasons filled with synergistic relationships and people connected to the purpose they have been called by God to fulfill. Some believers will live their lives never having understood why they were here on earth.

Some believers will pass on with all of their talents, God-given gifts, and potential buried with them. Some will even make lots of money, but it will either disappear just as quickly as it arrives or never accomplish what it was purposed for. Why? Because although they accepted Jesus Christ's salvation, they did not receive or implement His kingdom plan throughout all the areas of their lives. Tithing is a part of this plan. God is definitely willing and able to bless us. If we want God's kind of prosperity, which means nothing missing or broken in our lives, it is necessary for us to embrace God's plan for provision by making tithing and giving a priority in our lives.

Chapter 2
The Case for Tithing

Before I take you through the tithing testimonies of my life, I'd like to share some foundational scriptures around the principle of tithing. My hope is that as I build my case for tithing, the information will help to dispel some myths you've heard or strengthen your understanding of this important principle. Let's take a look at where tithing comes from.

Tithing Existed *before* the Ten Commandments

Tithing is a principle that God first modeled in Genesis 2 and first mentioned in Genesis 14. God establishes many truths and principles that we live by today in this first book of the Bible. Here we see God showing us how and to whom we should submit our tithes and what He does upon receipt of our tithes and offerings. Genesis chapter 14 discusses the meeting between the High Priest Melchizedik and Abram, servant of God. In those days, it was tradition to bring a "tithe" of all to the High Priest of the land. Giving is an act of praise, worship, and thanksgiving. This was one way the Israelites honored God. Abram gave Melchizedik a tithe of all he had, and Melchizedik blessed Abram in return. God blessed His people with everything they had. These blessings included their lives, their families, their flocks, their herbs and spices, their land, and their overall prosperity. God blessed Abram one hundred percent. Abram in return gave a tithe, also known as a tenth, of all he had to show God that he was grateful and that although the people and things he was blessed with were valuable to him, they were not God over him. By giving the tithe of all he had, Abram acknowledged and honored God as his source and his sustainer.

Tithing Is an Everlasting Covenant

Melchizedik was the High Priest of Abraham's time. One of the High Priest's responsibilities in those days was to collect the tithe and offering. Abraham and Melchizedik have passed on. Hebrews 6:20 says that Jesus Christ is our High Priest forever because He lives forever. So now, in the modern day, we submit our tithes and offerings to the local church. The priest, pastor, or shepherd of that house is responsible for utilizing the money in a way that benefits God's kingdom, the house of God, and that honors our High Priest, Jesus Christ.

Some people believe that tithing is an Old Testament principle. However, the reference to the order of Melchizedik in the New Testament further proves two things: 1) Jesus Christ came to fulfill the law and bring principles to life, and 2) The scripture confirms that tithing is not bound by time. It was established by God in the Old Testament and is still relevant to the believer today. There was just a "changing of the guards" from Melchizedik, an earthly, finite High Priest, to a Heavenly, Everlasting High Priest who is Jesus Christ.

Money vs. Faith

Tithing is more about faith than it is about money. Hebrews 11:6 states, "Without faith, it's impossible to please God." Not just faith in God when we understand, but faith in God even when we don't. Not faith in God when we know how the story will end; faith in God when the story is unpredictable. Faith is everything. Without it, we fail; we remain stagnant, digress, or go around in circles. Without it, we roam in the wilderness for years and years. Without it, we can't see past our current circumstances. Without it, we live in fear of what tomorrow will bring. Without faith, we cannot receive the blessings of God. But with faith, oh my Lord! We can move mountains; we can receive divine restoration, healing, and promotion; we can break generational curses, generate testimonies that will bring others to Christ, and defeat our adversaries with a prayer. Abraham and Sarah, Moses, Paul, Rahab, Joshua, and Samuel are all cited in the Bible because of their faith. The Bible says in Romans 4:3 that they believed God or had faith in God and "it was accounted to them for righteousness." Having faith in God by believing His word and operating by Godly principles puts us in right standing with Him. Tithing is an act of faith. It says, "Lord, I will trust you," "Lord, you are my source." Tithing says,

"Lord, you are Lord over me, not my money, my job, my bills, not my circumstances or the opinions of others."

God Wants a Tithe of All

Whenever God blesses us, and no matter what He blesses us with, He wants us to honor Him by giving the tithe back to Him. There are 168 hours in a week. There are 1,440 minutes in a day. For every brand-new day, we should "tithe" by spending a portion of our day with Him, thanking Him and giving Him praise. Out of a seven-day week, we should "tithe" by spending some time each week in the house of God, listening to sound teaching and being built up in our faith. Our talents, gifts, abilities, and resources belong to God. We should "tithe" by blessing God and His people with these resources and abilities. Like my pastor always says, "God keeps GOOD books!" He remembers our faithfulness. God blesses us and multiplies all we have when we make conscious choices to honor Him with all we have. Nothing is too small, so faithfully give what you do have. Little becomes much in the hand of the Lord.

Tithing Is a Covenant Thing

There will be believers who flourish in God's kingdom because they enter into covenant with God. Their lives will be examples of faith and show forth God's glory. They will have the capacity to bless in multiple ways and to be blessed in multiple ways. They will trample on lack and poverty. They will be victorious in every area of their lives. Because they have entered into covenant with the Most High God through tithing, they will hear the voice of God behind His word. God will whisper secrets, make crooked paths straight, and illuminate a road that will take you straight to where you need to be when you honor the tithing covenant. God wants us to walk into the fullness of His blessings. When we do not sow into the kingdom of God through tithing and offerings, we only receive *part* of what belongs to us as believers. Because God is tied to His word and cannot go against it, He cannot ignore what He has said about tithing. Malachi 3:10 makes it clear that tithing is a heavenly mandate and that for every man and woman under the sun who chooses to honor this covenant, a blessing surely awaits. Malachi 3:10 (NIV) states:

"Bring the whole tithe into the storehouse, that there may be food in my house. Test me in this," says the LORD Almighty, "and see if I will not throw open the floodgates of heaven and pour out so much blessing that there will not be room enough to store it."

As you can see, the tithe is designed to bless us continually. Tithing brings us into a place where the blessings we receive do not go in one door and out the other but instead they remain. They gain momentum. Before you know it, one blessing meets another blessing meets another blessing, and so on! This is the blessed life! This is harvest-to-harvest living. Tithing is designed to bless us to the point where we cannot store all of the blessings we have received. We become blessed to be a blessing. All of these blessings are not to be selfishly stored away. God wants to meet our needs, grant us the desires of our hearts, and show us who He wants *us* to bless as well. This is the beauty of having more than enough; you don't have to worry or be afraid of giving. You can be a blessing and not miss a beat! Prosperity in God's eyes means nothing missing and nothing broken. When we are in covenant with God, He works with us and for us to make sure that every area of our lives, including our walk of faith and our health, finances, relationships, and families align with His word and are made whole. This alignment brings God glory and bears witness to the fact that God cares for each and every one of His children. When we are blessed and our lives are in order, it shows forth God's goodness, God's mercy, and God's faithfulness. These attributes make us better witnesses to unbelievers and an encouragement to the Body of Christ.

When the life of a believer is fruitful, it declares over and over and over again that God is faithful. It shows that He is not a man that He should lie, and that if He says it and we honor it, if He says it and we do it, only blessings will follow our choice to obey, honor, and trust in His word. Be encouraged by Numbers 23:19, which says:

God is not a man, that He should lie, nor a son of man that He should repent. Has He said, and will He not do? Or has He spoken, and will He not make it good?

And the answer is YES. If God said it, He will make it good.

God Can Be Touched by Sacrificial Giving

Consistently honoring God by giving our tithes and offerings is definitely a sacrifice. It's not convenient or easy. There are always other interests, needs, and wants to contend with. Always. Most people work hard for the money they earn. Just to give 10 percent, even though we still have 90 percent left, still takes fortitude and conviction. We have to believe that sowing seed through tithes and offerings will only bring blessings. We must also believe that these blessings will supersede the sacrifice itself. Solomon embodied this belief.

Let's take a look at 1 Kings 3:4-5 which says:

*Now the king went to Gibeon to sacrifice there, for that was the great high place: Solomon offered **a thousand burnt offerings** on that altar. At Gibeon the Lord appeared to Solomon in a dream by night; and God said, "Ask! What shall I give you?"*

An uncommon offering given with the right spirit granted Solomon uncommon access to God. God was so pleased by Solomon's sacrifice that He not only gave him the wisdom he requested but also riches and honor. The wisdom, wealth, and honor Solomon acquired from God exceeded that of all the kings who had ever walked the earth, including his father King David. Yes, God filled a spiritual void in Solomon, a king who already had more than enough financially. This goes to show that no matter where you are in life, whether you are in a low-income household, middle class, wealthy, or in the upper-most echelon of our society, God can still meet your need right where you are. For the millionaires and billionaires who are reading this book, God's plan for provision is for you too! You might be thinking, what more could Solomon have needed? He seemed to have everything! Well, you know just as well as I do that there are many things money cannot buy. Solomon knew that he could not rely on the world's system for wisdom. He had an entire kingdom that would now hang on his every word. He was inexperienced and knew that only God could guide him and help him to be a wise and understanding ruler. Maybe you are also thinking that Solomon *did* buy his way to more wisdom. The truth is that Solomon humbly sacrificed something that was extremely valuable to show God that he was willing to lay it all down just to please and receive direction from Him. Through his giving, Solomon testified that God was God over him and the Giver of all blessings—spiritual and financial. It was clear that Solomon's abundant resources or his connections to the dignitaries of his kingdom were not his sources of provision. Because of his sacrificial offering, God granted Solomon access to His divine plan for provision, met his need for wisdom and understanding, and then some.

Promises Linked with Tithing

There are numerous benefits for tithing believers. Have you ever received a sum of money that seemed to have run out superfast without really meeting the need you had? The Bible says in Malachi 3:11 that God will rebuke the devourer. He will not allow the adversary to "poke holes in our baskets." Have you ever had something yanked away from you that you really wanted or needed? Did this cost you extra time or money, or bring grief? God says that He will restore the years that the locust, cankerworm, and the caterpillar have stolen (Joel 2:25). Do you ever feel like what you have is never enough? God says, give and it shall be given unto you, good measure, pressed down, shaken together, and running over, shall men pour into your bosom (Luke 6:38). Malachi 3:8 holds one of the biggest promises God ever made concerning tithing. As a matter of fact, most of the Scripture is God's promise to us. It says:

Bring ye all the tithes into the storehouse, that there may be meat in mine house, **and prove me now, says the LORD of Hosts, if I will not open you the windows of heaven, and pour you out a blessing, that there shall not be room enough to receive it. And I will rebuke the devourer for your sakes, and he shall not destroy the fruits of your ground; neither shall your vine cast her fruit before the time in the field, says the LORD of hosts. And all nations shall call you blessed; for ye shall be a delightsome land, says the Lord of hosts.**

Now, did you get all that? This Scripture is no joke! God put Himself on the line and said "Prove me now!" He's basically saying, "C'mon and test Me! Give me what you have and see if I won't make more out of it! Give Me a reason to open the flood-gates in your life! I dare you!" That's pretty bold, huh? Well, we serve a bold God. We just need to take Him at His word. The premise of this scripture is not only abundance. In these two verses, God promises productivity, protection, and timeliness. He will ensure that your fruit (the blessing God produces in your life) is timely and beneficial. He won't allow your fruit to grow in the wrong season. He will give you wisdom on when to invest, with whom, and how much. He will steer you away from ideas, initiatives, and people who don't have your best interest at heart. Remember, the devourer has a plan for our money too. In this scripture, God promises not to let the "devourer" destroy everything that you worked so hard to build. This means that He will protect your family, your business ventures, your finances, your mind, and your health **and** cause them to flourish.

Tithing empowers us to prosper in all things. It goes beyond financial resources. When believers give tithes and offerings, they open up a bank account in Heaven and are able to humbly tap on God's shoulder and remind Him of His promises in Malachi chapter 3. When things aren't lining up right and seem to be just plain old out of order, a tithing believer can rest assured that God will deliver them and get them out of the situation that has them bound. Tithing believers have access to these promises. I pray that you are getting closer to making a commitment to sow your tithes, offerings, and sacrificial gifts today. So now it's time to come with me on a journey down testimony lane. I will show you how faithful God has shown Himself to be and how each of His promises has come to fruition in my life because my family and I decided to consistently honor the tithing covenant. First, I'll share a little about where it all began.

Chapter 3
The Backstory

At age sixteen, I was a junior in high school and was working to recover from BAS (Bad Attitude Syndrome). I had made terrible decisions at the age of fifteen, which caused me a lot of grief during my junior year. I had cut so many classes, which resulted in my failing most of them. I was burdened with the dilemma of needing more credits than I had time to earn. I had six more semesters of credits to earn with only four semesters left. In an attempt to make up as many credits as possible, I had to sign up for summer school, afterschool, and Saturday school. During the general school day, I had eight classes straight with no lunch in my schedule. I did this for two semesters. I was absolutely worn out and exhausted. But I had to pay the price for the poor choices I had made.

I heard a buzz around campus about a specialized program that allowed students to work for pay and earn credits in school at the same time. I applied for and was accepted into the Cooperative Learning program. Because of the supportive way in which the program was structured, along with the high level of accountability, I began to soar academically. The director saw something in me that I didn't even see in myself. So she chose me. I began to work for a Fortune 500 company as an intern while making up all the credits I was missing. My high school senior advisor told me that I should apply to a two-year college because of my failing GPA. I didn't take her advice. My family believed that I could do better than that and since my brother had been accepted into New Paltz for the previous school year, they encouraged me to apply to SUNY New Paltz through the same program. So I applied. I wrote my own essay and trusted God. I received an envelope from New Paltz in May stating that I had been accepted to the institution. Boy was I ecstatic! At this time in my life, I actually started to believe more and more that if I honored God with everything I had, big or small, He would surely remember me when it mattered most.

Chapter 4

Tithing Testimony #1 Crooked Paths Made Straight

I started attending New Paltz the summer after I graduated from high school. I completed my first year of college and continued to work with the company that I worked for in high school during the summer breaks. I had a year of college experience, so the company gave me a raise from $8.00 an hour to $9.83 an hour. I was so grateful because back in those days eight dollars was already two dollars and twenty-five cents above minimum wage and they still gave me almost two dollars an hour above that. I had no real expenses and I really liked my job. Every two weeks I would get paid and give tithes and offerings to the church I was attending at the time. And of course, I couldn't resist doing a little...or a lot of shopping! I mean I *was* a college girl with a J-O-B! One Monday morning, I came in to work as usual and checked in with my supervisor. There were a lot of new faces on the floor. I found out that these new faces were college students who had just started a summer internship with my company. According to my supervisor, this group of interns was set to receive a salary of $17.00 an hour. Although my supervisor was happy to hear about this, she was concerned that I had been there before them and that they would be earning almost double what I earned. She really didn't mention anything to me about it after that point and I didn't bring it up. I told myself that maybe they came from very prestigious colleges and universities—which they did. I also told myself that they were most likely more qualified than I was, since they had been hired to complete a specific task connected to engineering—which they were. I didn't have a background in engineering or computer science. I carried on and did what I was asked, day in and day out. I even helped the new interns get acclimated to their new roles and our office space. A few days had passed when my supervisor called me up and asked me to come to her floor. When I got to her desk, she was on the phone so I looked out from the ninety-seventh floor of the World Trade Center to *try* to calm my nerves. Ha! Who does that? Well, I did. A million questions ran through my mind. Would they fire me since I wasn't majoring in engineering? Was today my last day? She finally ended her conversation and began to explain that she had spoken to her supervisor. She told them about me, my history with the company, and my current salary. She asked them if they could increase my salary to the same hourly rate as the interns. They said YES! At that moment I felt like I could fly. She told me that they would pay me retroactive pay as well for the month I worked at the old hourly rate. I also had the opportunity to earn overtime, which was $25.50 an hour. It was at this moment that I realized God is always working on our behalf. If you are grateful and continue to sow seeds through tithes and offerings, God will make every crooked path straight and He will right every wrong.

Sometimes God even lays it on people's hearts to fight or advocate on our behalf, so much so that we don't have to lift a finger…Well, except to put our tithes and offerings in the collection plate.

Chapter 5

Tithing Testimony #2
Divine Direction

When I was nineteen years old, I applied for and was accepted into a study abroad program. This had not been a desire of mine for any extent of time. The Lord just dropped it into my spirit and sent people to encourage me to take this opportunity.

I spoke to a few students who had studied in Besançon, France during the previous semester. In January 2001, I prepared to board a plane to France.

My family and close friends accompanied me to the airport. We took pictures, hugged, kissed, embraced, laughed, and then said our six-month goodbyes. I went through security as they watched and I waved goodbye. It was one of the saddest and most bittersweet moments of my life. I took my carryon bag out of the scanning tub, walked around the corner, found a quiet space, and cried like a baby. I believed that I would return home, but I knew it was far away from tomorrow. So I cried and cried until it was time to board the plane. For the first month, I didn't really speak much. I knew enough French to order food and to purchase a cell phone and a calling card. I took French classes every day. One day as

I was sitting in my dorm room alone, I began to think about how I would explain all that I had learned in France to my family. I thought about how I would teach them French. It really wasn't anything deep, but at this moment the Lord planted a thought into my spirit. "Teach." I had never in my life thought of becoming a teacher. From the time I was ten years old, I had declared that I would become a lawyer. I liked to debate and argue different points. Until this moment, I believed I was an advocate and that I was destined to become a lawyer. The Holy Spirit spoke to me and gave me a clear sense of direction in a totally unplanned way. Now, you may ask, what does this have to do with tithing? Well, the Bible says seek ye first the kingdom of God and His righteousness and all other things will be added unto you. When you sow through your tithes and offerings, you are seeking God's kingdom and His way of doing things first. Therefore, all other things fall into place. "All other things" include wisdom, direction, guidance, peace, liberty, joy, and the like. The phrase "all other things" represents any need or desire you may have in your life. The beautiful thing is that when you are aligned with God's word, the Lord will step right in to bless you with whatever you need because you have already sought His kingdom first and honored His word. Tithing and offering is a part of the kingdom plan. You can't go wrong when you honor God's system for sowing and reaping.

Chapter 6

Tithing Testimony #3
God Opens Doors

Now that the Holy Spirit had tugged on my heart and inspired and encouraged me to be a teacher, a great dilemma ensued. I was twenty years old, in my junior year of undergrad, and a communication major. Huh? How would I become a teacher when I had taken not even ONE course in education? Uh…God? How in the world am I going to become a teacher? Well, when you've got seed in good ground with faith and purpose attached to it, God makes a way to get what you need to you. My father is the greatest. He's the kind of person you can talk to about anything. I was in a dim, old college dorm room in Besançon, France when God spoke to my heart about this major shift. I called and shared the vision with my dad. He was supportive and is one of the main people God used in my life to help me get to where I am today. He believed that I would be great and that I could do it. That was all I needed to hear.

After I completed my study-abroad coursework requirements, it was time to return to Brooklyn for summer vacation. My father thought it would be a good idea to hit the ground running and try to figure out how I was going to become a teacher. There was no doubt in his mind that there was a way. We visited one of the district offices in East New York, Brooklyn. I knew just based on my study-abroad experience that I wanted to come back and serve the East New York community where I'd spent the majority of my childhood years. I wanted to have an opportunity to tell the children from my community that they could go further than the moon, study abroad, and live their dreams. So we went to the office in our local community looking for a way in. We met a gentleman who was a veteran in the school system. He knew the system in and out and was very helpful. He asked me some questions about my background and what my major was. He asked me what my GPA was. It was above a 3.0. When he heard my GPA, it was almost as if a lightbulb went off in his head. He asked if I'd ever heard about a recently launched alternative teacher certification program and of course I had not. He began to explain some of the criteria and told me that based on my educational background and current GPA, I would definitely be eligible to apply. After our conversation, I left that office with some pep in my step and glide in my stride. I was so excited to know that there was an alternative way to get into the teaching profession. I went online as the district representative had recommended and looked up the program. I read all the information over and over again. I wanted to make sure I was not missing anything. I had to apply by mid-October online. Then they would notify me of whether or not I was accepted as an initial applicant and if I would be able to advance to the next part of the interview phase. I stayed up at New Paltz and completed applications for two programs that offered alternative ways to obtain teaching certificates. There were thousands of applicants.

To make a long story short, I was accepted into the program. My father had another bright idea a couple of months before the school year began. He thought we should go hunting for nearby schools so that I wouldn't have to be placed in a school that would require me to spend four hours a day commuting. We walked to the nearest school, which was only three minutes away by foot. We walked in and were greeted by the assistant principal. She knew my father because one of my younger sisters attended the school years ago. She asked us what we needed and I told her that I had recently been accepted into a teaching program and was looking for placement. She immediately informed me that the principal was leery of folks who entered the teaching profession through my program. Two had left their students without teachers in the middle of the school year. Despite her knowledge of the principal's reluctance to hire anyone from my program, the assistant principal asked us to have a seat in the conference room. We did. A few minutes later, the assistant principal came back to tell me that the principal would see me. My father stayed in the conference room and I walked across the hall to the principal's office. The main office was such a busy place. I waited behind the counter until I was called. The principal called me in and asked me to have a seat. Boy was she a tough cookie! From the moment I sat down to the moment I walked out, she grilled me. I mean, boy did she grill me. She asked me if I was sure this was what I wanted to do. I told her I most definitely was. I told her that I didn't think of it as just a job but a calling.

At that moment a student knocked on the door to tell her that two fifth-graders had just gotten into a fight on the third floor. After the student left, she looked at me and said, "Are you sure this is what you want to do? Do you see what I mean?" I told her I had taught dance one summer and that I taught Sunday School. I told her that I knew I could do it and I wanted to give back by teaching in a school in my community. She told me about the two teachers who had left during the school year and how devastated she was about how it all played out. I told her I had no intention of bailing out in the middle of the school year and that I would stick it out. Finally, she said "OK." It wasn't filled with excitement but that was OK because at that moment I had enough excitement for both of us. I got the job! This was the first school, first interview, and three minutes' walking distance from my house. I got the job! Hallelujah! I tried to maintain my composure as the principal signed my placement paper, which stated that I would be a full-time teacher at this school in a few short months.

Guess what? That's not all! You want to know what else God orchestrated? Well, I'm so glad you asked! This is the school where I met my husband. His first year was the previous year. I started teaching in September, we went on our first date in December, got engaged in June and were married the following February. We are still here eight years later... still tithing, giving, believing, serving, and trusting God. Hallelujah!

So, do see what I mean? When you are in covenant with God through faithfully serving Him and giving your tithes and offering, He not only addresses financial needs but He grants you the desires of your heart and makes sure that you are at the right place at the right time to receive a blessing that He designed just for you. This is what God's plan for provision is all about. He wants us to be whole in all areas of our lives. C'mon...Isn't God AMAZING?

Now remember, this opportunity came during my last semester in college. I didn't have much money at all. Whenever I did get a few dollars, I gave an offering. Sometimes we do have "dry spells" in our lives. God knows our hearts. You can't give 10 percent of what you don't have. But when you've constantly honored the tithing covenant and given to God's kingdom when you had it to give, you always have seed in the ground. If you keep a good, Godly attitude and water your seeds by meditating on and saying the word of God daily, you will still reap a harvest. God is always working on our behalf. I hope you've at least taken your seed out of your wallet or bank account by now! When you are obedient to God's word and confess the word only, you are in a prime position to receive a blessing. These blessings come in all different shapes and sizes. God is looking for covenant people. God is looking for people who will honor His word above their circumstances, the world's system, and the opinions and thoughts of other people. Tithing is a part of God's plan for provision. Believers who tithe faithfully become conduits for God's abundant blessings.

Chapter 7
Tithing Testimony #4 Double for Your Trouble!

Well, of course I'm biased because I'm writing this book, but I think this story is going to blow your mind! I can truly say that when it seems to us that there is no way, God is right there MAKING a way. That's what's so great about God, He is THE Creator and He is A Creator. My husband and I had been faithfully sowing into our ministry and other ministries that God laid on our hearts. We were just minding our own business, being faithful with our words, deeds, and money. Children of God, if we want "the more" that God has for us, we must be faithful in good times, so-so times, and bad times. Sometimes we get so close to becoming a miracle, so close to our turnaround, and because we can't "see" it, or because it doesn't feel like it, we stop believing, we stop praying, we stop decreeing, we stop praising God for what He is going to do. Please, please don't stop! I think if we could see a video of all the times in life we have turned our back on God's word because we let our faith fail, if it showed us how many inches away we were from our breakthrough, we would kick ourselves! Stay faithful.

So, let's get to the story. Like I said, we were being faithful, sowing, serving, believing, and being about God's business. We were sitting in church one day and my pastor began to make an appeal for a special offering. Now, this is uncharacteristic of our church as we only collect one offering every Sunday and Wednesday. We don't have the offering for the usher board, deacon board, chicken-frying committee, or communion committee. We just collect one offering. So my pastor stood flatfooted and said, "God wants to give you double for your trouble! For those of you who sow what God has laid on your heart today, in ninety days God is going to give you double!" My husband and I sowed a seed for two hundred and fifty dollars. It was our best gift and what God had laid on our hearts. You see, the foundation of sowing and reaping is obedience. We must be obedient and hear the voice of God when He tells us what to do, what to give, and who to give to. Don't you know our blessings are hinged upon this premise? If God says to sow ten thousand dollars, don't give ten dollars. On the flip side, if he says to give five hundred dollars, don't give a thousand.

We sowed the seed for the amount that the Lord laid on our hearts. Our pastor and his wife laid hands on the gifts and prayed over them. Church ended. We left the sanctuary believing that God would do more than exceedingly, abundantly above all we could ever ask or think, but we had no idea of how much he would bless us. When we got home, I counted ninety days on my calendar and marked the date, which was the first week of February. We continued to be faithful in our giving and in our walk with God.

Here's a little side note: while you are believing God for "the more," you absolutely, positively must be faithful over what you already have (Matthew 25:23). Now I know you might be asking, so, you never had any other issues going on? You never had to use the tithes for something else? Of course! Within our years of serving the Lord we've had all sorts of financial issues arise...many. We have had family issues, money issues, house issues, job issues, but our pastor taught us through the word of God that sowing through tithes, offerings, and other God-ordained gifts such as first-fruit offerings are the way OUT. You cannot get out of any situation sent to destroy your life and your relationship with God by breaking God's covenant. If you want God to get you out, to fight for you, to advocate for you, to represent you, to make your enemies your footstool, to prosper you in ALL areas of your life, then you must honor His way, His system, His way of doing things, His methodology, and forsake your own. The Bible says,

This foolish plan of God is wiser than the wisest of human plans, and God's weakness is stronger than the greatest of human strength. (1 Corinthians 1:25 NLT)

To some this may seem futile and like plain ol' crazy talk. But I am telling you, when God digs you out of your mess, you are OUT. When God makes the crooked paths straight in your life, they are straight. For as long as we honor Him with our ways and put His word above our own understanding and deduction of how we think things should go, we won't go back to how things used to be. Whew! I was preaching myself happy there. I digress. Let's go back to the story.

We marked the calendar, continued to sow and pray and be faithful right through our trials. If we missed a tithe payment for whatever reason, we made it up as soon as we could. During this time, I was an elementary school teacher. What a wonderful experience! I was in my classroom one morning and I felt the Holy Spirit tugging on me. He told me that I wasn't going to be "here" for much longer. At the time, I had no idea what the "here" meant. I didn't know if He meant here in the classroom, here in the school, or both, but I had a feeling it had something to do with my next assignment. Life went on as usual. Nothing fell out of the sky, nor did an angel appear to me. All you need to activate the power of God's word is faith. All you need to deactivate the power of His word in your life is unbelief. The Bible says in Ephesians 3:20 that *God is able to do exceedingly, abundantly, above all we could ever ask or think.* Now, get this…He does this *according to the POWER that works in us.* You've got to be obedient and have faith on the inside of you to connect with God's word in order for the fruit of God's word to manifest on the outside. When God said it, I believed. I didn't know all the details and I didn't need to. I knew that the God who spoke to me was a more than credible source. Since I knew that God's desire was always for me to prosper and have all things good and godly, I was not afraid of his plan for my future. The word says in Jeremiah 29:11, *I know the thoughts I think towards you, says the Lord, thoughts of peace and not of evil, to give you a future and a hope (an expected end).* A few months after I heard this message, we came home from a long day of work. I picked up the mail pile, which had some bills, a teacher's union newspaper, and some junk mail. As always, I laid the mail on the table, kicked off my shoes, sat down, and started relaxing. I picked up the newspaper from the dining room table and began to read the stories and various advertisements. Nothing stood out. It was just more of the same. Three weeks later, after moving the newspaper from place to place, I picked it up again and flipped through it as if it were the first time I was reading it. I came across an advertisement for an organization that trained educators to become principals in urban schools. I hadn't seen the advertisement before and I hadn't heard of the organization before either.

I did remember hearing the voice of the Lord back in my classroom. I felt the Lord speaking to me so strongly at that moment. I was sitting on my living room floor just gazing at this advertisement. There were featured schools that did something great, union issues, teaching tips, and the like. I put the newspaper down and just left it. I didn't throw it away. Now let me make something clear, I do not like clutter at all! I can't stand bunches of piles of papers everywhere. So usually with the first opportunity to identify something as junk mail, insignificant mail, not-now mail, or obsolete mail, I throw it in the garbage. But it was not so with this newspaper. I'm thinking, "Lord, Noooooo! You want me to become a principal? You want me to be a school leader?" I was a fourth-year teacher and that was all the experience I had as an educator besides teaching Sunday School. "Lord, you want ME to be a principal?" I was twenty-five years old, and I had taught at one school under two administrators. That was it. That was all. I was stunned at God's proposition. I am not going to tell you that when the Lord revealed his plan for me I ran around the house yelling and thanking Him, because I did not. I was shocked. I was never a teacher leader, barely a mentor; I was just Jubilee Mosley, a third-grade teacher. Well, I later found out (later meaning within the next hour or so) that God didn't care about my lack of experience. He cared about my heart for children. He cared about my level of commitment and faithfulness in ministry and at my place of employment. He cared about me upholding His covenant and keeping His word. I took the newspaper and went down to my basement where the computer was. I logged on and visited the website of the organization. I found out what the criteria were for applicants and when the informational session would be held.

The next morning, I told my husband what the Lord showed me about my professional future.

He encouraged me and told me that I should go for it. I moved forward and took a giant leap of faith. Although, I was filled with nervousness I knew that somehow God was going to sustain me. I made it to the informational meeting. The attendees all held various positions within education. During the Q&A segment, one potential applicant asked how we would be scored or graded and the facilitator said, "We do not compare scores. We accept anyone who is able to demonstrate these capacities as listed on the criteria form. You are basically competing against your best selves." Hmmmph! That was all I needed to hear!

Now, let me just say that this organization was very, very selective. They received tens of thousands of applications and only 7 percent of applicants were accepted. But it was encouraging to know that *they* were not even concerned about my years of experience. They were concerned about my alignment with their mission and vision and whether or not I could have a positive impact on the lives of children as a school leader. So, I applied. There were three stages to the application process. I submitted my online application and was advanced to the next round, which was a one-on-one interview. I had to request a letter of recommendation from my principal. I thought she would be supportive, but at the time she was not. After reading the recommendation, she pulled me into her office, slammed the door, and asked me if I really thought I could be a principal after four years of teaching. Now, this was someone who was always in my corner, encouraging me to be the very best teacher I could be. She has inspired me in so many ways. I was so shocked because she seemed irate and expressed that this was just not something that could be done. She told me that she wouldn't be able to recommend me for the program because it was way out of my reach and way too soon in my career. I was taken aback and discouraged by her response. I was just doing what God told me. I didn't wake up one day and decide that this was what I wanted to do. She handed over my recommendation and on it she wrote that I was a solid teacher but that she would not recommend anyone who had only three years of teaching experience to become a principal. I had to submit this statement because every applicant was required to submit a recommendation from his or her current principal or supervisor. So I sealed the envelope and submitted it. I told my husband what had occurred and he encouraged me. We went over to my parents' house and they encouraged me as well. So, as quickly as it happened, I just as quickly got over it. There will always be naysayers, but it's not our responsibility to change their minds or prove them wrong. I just tried to make sure I did not allow their words and negative confessions to weigh me down and change my God-ordained course.

Sometimes you don't realize how big and out of this world your dreams are until you tell other people or show them where you are going. I received a notification a few weeks later that I had advanced to the final interview stage. The interview was scheduled from 8:00 a.m. to 6:00 p.m. The organization wanted applicants to experience an interview similar to the day in the life of a principal. This interview process was beyond intense. Thank God for the Holy Spirit. If you are reading this book and you're unsaved, it is my prayer and hope that you will say the prayer of salvation at the back of this book and then ask God for the gift of the Holy Spirit and the prayer language. The Holy Spirit is Jesus Christ in spirit. He is our comforter and He guides me every day. Thank God for the Holy Spirit, who was with me every step of the way. I was the last one to enter the conference room where the first part of the interview would be held. The other applicants said "Good morning" and seemed friendly, so that was helpful. It helped me feel a little less anxious but, truth be told, I was so nervous. It was only the Lord who helped me not to shake or tremble. I reviewed the agenda for the day and realized I had a few more minutes before we had to begin the marathon. I had been praying and praying and praying. I asked the Lord to use me, to grant me His favor, and to be in my mouth. I excused myself from the conference room and went to the restroom. I paced and prayed, prayed and paced. My prayer went something like this: "Lord, I don't know what I am doing. Please help me. I am here because you told me to come. Be in my mouth. Speak through me because I don't know what I am doing. Lord, no matter what happens I will give you the praise." I fixed myself up, got myself together, squared my back, and went back to the conference room. I sat down and didn't really engage in much conversation. In walked about ten or twelve interviewers, which at that time seemed like an entire army of people. Sheesh! They sat around the perimeter of the conference table, introduced themselves, and asked us to introduce ourselves by saying our names, schools, and roles. Ha! This was going to be interesting. So of course some people used the opportunity to share their many titles, of which I had none! When it was my turn, I said, "Good morning, I'm Jubilee Mosley and I'm a third-grade teacher in Brooklyn." Take that, devil! I will not try to be something I'm not. I believe if you allow Him to, God can and will work with you and through you, WHEREVER you are. He doesn't need our professional resumes because He is God. Now, I am absolutely a proponent for upward mobility and education. In fact, one of my favorite things to do is to graduate! However, this does not replace my dire need for God or relieve me from the call to honor His system and love Him with all my heart. If you are saved, then you are part of God's kingdom, which is God's way of doing things. This means that our mindsets have to shift to align with God's word and His expectations. He needs us to be in line with His covenant. The world says, "Pay your bills, save some money, buy the things you want, and then maybe you can give some 'charitable' gifts if you have any left." The world says, "Get all you can, then CAN all you get!" God's system says, "Pay your Godly bill (tithe) so that My work can be done on the earth and so that you will never be in need. Then, pay your bills, save, and make purchases within reason." God says we can MAKE our way prosperous (Joshua 1:8) by meditating on and honoring His word. By doing so, we receive access to Godly ideas, insight, favor, synergistic relationships, and the like.

God is looking for covenant people who honor His word and system above all else. If you are faithful and honor God's covenant concerning your finances, God will surely bless you. This is why it didn't matter that I wasn't ready to move toward school administration based on the world's system or mainstream mindsets. According to God's system, I was ready for promotion because I was in covenant with Him and faithful to His word. I was spiritually in the right place at the right time. Now don't get me wrong, I am not bragging. My husband and I were still trying to make lemonade with the lemons life had handed to us throughout this process BUT we still kept our eyes on God. Honestly, we couldn't have made it if we didn't. He is faithful even when we are not. He is amazing! We continued to honor Him. You don't have to be perfect. You just have to love God and demonstrate your love by being consistent and faithful concerning the things of God. Let's continue with the testimony.

After our introductions, the interview began. This was the tensest, most grueling interview process I had ever experienced in my life. We were watched and drilled on our pedagogical, supervisory, and administrative knowledge and insight from 8:00 a.m. until around 6:00 p.m. They did give us a marvelous lunch and some short breaks in between, so God bless them for that! I used every break they gave us to go to the bathroom and pray. Now, I'm not trying to be super-spiritual. I just know that God is my source. He is the One who equips me and gives me the grace to do all that He has called me to do. I knew that if I wanted to experience God's favor, goodness, and mercy, I would have to continue to seek Him first and consult Him continually throughout the day. I needed His help for sure! This is how I kept my peace of mind throughout this very trying day.

Finally, the interview day came to end. I met one-on-one with a member of the interview committee. She asked some questions and told me what the next steps would be. She told me I'd hear from them in about four weeks. It was one of those interviews that just left you out there. I wondered what they thought and how I did overall. Well, it didn't make any sense to wonder about it because I wouldn't know for a few more weeks. So I continued living, praising God, giving, and trusting in Him.

Several weeks later, I was in Atlanta, Georgia with my former principal and two colleagues at a professional development seminar. I was so honored to have been selected to attend. I loved learning and sharing ideas with fellow teachers, so this was a prime opportunity for me. One day after a workshop, we were in the hotel browsing and trying to figure out what we were going to eat when my phone rang. It was one of the leaders from the organization I had interviewed with. She began to tell me that they were impressed by me during the interview and wanted to offer me one of the nine slots to be filled for this selection round. They wanted to train me to be a principal and a change agent. What? Who, me? Really? I wanted to drop my cell phone and run around that hotel lobby at least five times, screaming. I didn't, though. I didn't want the hotel staff to call security on me and have me escorted out. So I praised God in my hotel room instead! I mean…isn't God awesome? He is so good to us.

So, I know you're probably wondering what this acceptance meant. Well, it meant that I would work full-time as a principal intern while participating in a fully paid, full- time residency. The residency was all-expense-paid for coursework, course materials, and lodging and transportation for seminars. All residents were required to participate in a six-week summer foundation course. During this year-long residency, I would earn a certificate that would allow me to be a principal or assistant principal in any public, private, or charter school ranging from pre-kindergarten to twelfth grade. It also meant that my salary would go from about $40,000 to about $80,000 to 97,000+ in the following years. Can you say DOUBLE for your TROUBLE? You see, my husband and I gave an offering (sowed a seed) for $250, received the word from my pastor, and believed the word of God concerning the seed we had sown. God gave the increase and brought forth a harvest in our lives in due season. Did you notice that the size of the harvest exceeded the size of the seed sown? However, the size of the harvest matched our faith level concerning the seed we sowed. Again, the scripture says, *The Lord is able to do exceedingly abundantly above all you could ever ask or think...according to the power that works in us.* Don't worry about the size of your seed. Just make sure the amount you sow is the amount God said to sow. If you've got peace about it, sow it. When you hear a word from the Lord that speaks directly to your situation, sow it. We sowed a seed in addition to our tithes and offerings. When you honor the tithing covenant, God opens up other opportunities for you to sow cheerfully in faith and reap bountifully. Oh yes...and remember, seeds don't just sprout up into a plant in the same moment they are sown. Reaping a harvest takes a bit of patience as well. Don't be discouraged if it takes a little time (or a lot of time) to sprout. Just keep believing that your harvest is on its way. It will come in due season. Galatians 6:9 puts it like this:

So let's not get tired of doing what is good. At just the right time we will reap a harvest of blessing if we don't give up. (NLT)

When God says it's harvest time, it's HARVEST TIME and no one can stop it! Look what God did for us. God granted us access to the favor that comes with giving and within a matter of months, God not only gave us double for our trouble but also restored and catapulted us to the next level spiritually, financially, and professionally. To God be the glory!

Chapter 8
Tithing Testimony #5 When the Floodgates Open

During the summer course for the principal training, my husband fell ill. I spoke to him after a long day of classes and he told me to my surprise that he was in the emergency room. When he described the issue, I was saddened but not alarmed. Then I spoke with him once more after the doctor had seen him. The doctor said it was more urgent and dangerous than we thought. It turned out that my husband would have to undergo surgery to fix the problem. My emotions ran wild. Who would be with him? Why was this happening now? Yes. This book is still about tithing! My family tried to calm me down, which helped somewhat. I cried myself to sleep because my husband had been admitted to the hospital, I hadn't seen him in a month, I missed him, and I couldn't get to him. I had no additional funds because the "Double for My Trouble" raise wasn't due to kick in until September and we had just paid our mortgage. How in the world was I going to get home? I just prayed and asked God for peace and believed that He would make a way for me. Don't you know that God is God and can touch people's hearts and prompt them to bless you? Well, if you didn't…keep reading!

I called my program director and shared my issue with her through my tears. She asked me how I would be getting home and I told her that I would figure it out. I told her that once I did figure it out, I'd get back to her about when I would leave and return to complete the program. I was going to fly or take the train or bus. I wiped my face and walked outside to the common area of my suite. I don't know if it mattered that I wiped my face, since my eyes told the story of my dilemma. Two of my suitemates were there. I told them about my husband and that I would be leaving to go home but that I would return in a few days. They told me they would take notes for me so that I wouldn't be totally lost when I came back to class. I went back into my room and began to pray. I gave God praise, and asked Him to be with my husband and to help me get home to him. A few minutes later, I received a phone call from my program director. She told me that the organization would pay for a return flight from Boston to NYC. Just when I thought I couldn't cry anymore, here came the streams of tears, which, with the many, many "thank yous," expressed my deepest sentiments of gratitude. "Thank you Jesus! Thank You Lord!" Those were the only expressions I could muster up at that point. You would think my tear ducts were dry by now but they absolutely were not! I wiped my face again and walked out of my dorm room to be met by my roommate, whose room was on the other side of the suite. She walked toward me with a checkbook in her hand. She asked me how much a return ticket was from Boston to NYC. She began to write out a check to me. I told her the amount was about $130 and that the organization had already paid for my ticket to get home and back to Boston. She totally ignored me and kept writing out the check! She said, "Well, I already wrote it out! You can use this to buy whatever your husband will need in order to get better!" I will never forget that moment.

Let me just stop here and say that tithing is wonderful. The bank of Heaven is irreplaceable! Tithe consistently. Tithe on good days and not-so-good days. God will not allow us to go without. He will provide. We always keep seed in the ground because we just never know when we are going to need God's help. Sow your tithes, offerings, and gifts with great expectation. You may not believe you need God now, but like my pastor always says, "Just keep living!" The Bible says, *He will rebuke the hand of the devourer for your name's sake.* God will step in and turn your nothing into something if you remain in covenant with Him through tithing and honor His word as it relates to giving. That is what He did for my husband and me.

Back to the story...I began to pack up. The organization had worked with me to book both flights over the phone. News travels fast. As I was preparing to leave, I got a phone call from one of my colleagues, who, like many others, had become like family to me. He told me that the roommate who had given me the check had shared with him what happened. He wanted me to stop by the academic building where classes took place before I left for the airport. I agreed. I went over with luggage in hand and was met by my colleague, who is now more like an uncle to me. He said some words of encouragement and handed over an envelope filled with cash. He and my suitemate had informed my cohort of what happened. He said many of my cohort members were genuinely concerned and, though they were not asked to give, started to pull out money and asked that it be added to what he had given me. You want to talk about tears now? Boy, oh boy! I mean I was absolutely speechless! God amazed me. God can touch anybody's heart and cause people to bless you. I had only known this group of people for one month, but that was not enough to stop them from giving. I walked out of the building with my suitcase and several hundred dollars in cash. I flew out of Boston, went to the hospital to ensure my husband was OK and well taken care of, got him home safely, and flew back to Boston to finish my last week of coursework.

Let me just make it plain. If you work your seed, the seed will work for you. How do you do that? Make a conscious decision to serve God with your intellect, time, soul, will, emotions, spirit, AND your money! Sow like it's never going out of style because…it isn't! When you sow into the Kingdom of

God through your tithes and offerings, just remember that Heaven is really the City that never sleeps. Tithing is what allows you to receive the financial benefits of being a believer. Do you know that many believers live without these benefits? Just like a part-time or per diem employee may not have health or dental insurance or be fully vested into the retirement plan, so are non-tithing, non-sowing believers. They are not fully vested into God's system for provision through tithing. Until we do what God requires concerning our money, we can never truly say that He has our heart. The Bible says in Matthew 6:19:

Do not lay up for yourselves treasures on earth, where moth and rust destroy and where thieves break in and steal; but lay up for yourselves treasures in heaven, where neither moth nor rust destroys and where thieves do not break in and steal. For where your treasure is, there your heart will be also.

Like I said earlier, when you give your tithe and offering you are saying, God is my God and not my money. You are also saying, "Lord, thank you for being a provider. You are my source." I want to encourage you to become a Believer with Benefits and receive all the fringe benefits the Lord offers His children who not only confess His name but who are in covenant with Him through sowing tithes and offerings.

Chapter 9

Tithing Testimony #6 Rebuke the Devourer

In 2008, I was diagnosed with an aggressive form of breast cancer. I was twenty-six years old. My life changed instantly. But even in the midst of the storm, God showed me His awesome power and favor. Remember the principal-training organization I told you about earlier? Well, I was still in the process of being trained by them as a resident principal at the time of this diagnosis. I remember the call as though it just happened yesterday. I had gone for a biopsy and a breast sonogram a week earlier. The doctor called me back and asked that my husband and I come in to see her. I was so annoyed because I was so busy and knew that it would be hard for me to leave work to make it all the way over to where her office was. I was too busy. I decided to call her back and ask her to tell me what her concern was over the phone. I just knew that I was fine. I didn't understand why she would ask me to come all the way to her office when she could just tell me over the phone that the results of the biopsy were normal. I called the office and insisted I speak with her. She insisted I come in. I told her I wouldn't be able to make it in until later on in the week and she told me that I absolutely had to come in right away. She said, "Mosley, it doesn't look good…it's cancer." I tried to listen to everything else she said but I couldn't concentrate anymore. It was like the world had sped up and spun me around in a whirlwind. It all happened so fast. I called my husband but he couldn't answer because he was teaching. I called and called and called and while I called my husband, I also called on the name of Jesus because there really wasn't anyone else who could help me. I laid my hand on the area and I said, "Lord Jesus, you are the Healer. Please heal me. Please be My Healer!"

My husband sent me a text but I told him I couldn't share the news via text. I called my dad in the meantime. He answered and I had to share the devastating news with him. My husband called me and I had to share it once again. He left work and came to get me right away from the school where I was working at the time. I know, I know, you're probably wondering what this has to do with tithing. But trust me, I'm working on something. I'm setting it up! So anyway, after getting a second biopsy and a second opinion, vacillating within the worlds of fear and faith and prayer, I decided to go through with chemotherapy. This would mean that I would need to take a leave of absence. Having a job that provided an income and health and dental insurance was a very important thing. My husband and I had to pay our mortgage in addition to all the other bills associated with homeownership. We could not afford to lose half of our income. But thank God for the tithe and the teaching of the word of God. My pastor always reminded us that God is our source. I believe this wholeheartedly and through my life's circumstances realize that even though the scripture says, "money answers all things," money still has limitations when it does not have the hand of God or God's favor on it. God's touch on money causes it to flourish, grow, bless, thrive, regenerate, and build. God's touch on money causes it to be able to answer the "things" in our lives. I received a call from the executive director of my program. I had shared my diagnosis with the people I worked most closely with.

Honestly, I didn't plan on taking a break or a leave of absence. It was the barrage of doctors' visits, pre-operation testing, and the conversation with my executive director that catapulted me into reality and pushed me to change my mind. Her conversation helped me to realize that I didn't have to be "super-woman" or push myself to the limit; I could just go through the process, take my time, pray, and help my body heal. But what she said next really sealed the deal because it dismantled one of my biggest concerns—money. She said, "Jubilee, take the time off. Take about four weeks off to assess the situation and see how you feel after that. Don't worry about your pay or benefits; everything will stay intact. We'll talk in about a month or so and you can let me know if you need more time."

Beloved, beloved, beloved! Listen to me! Listen to me! Throughout this process, my husband and I never stopped tithing and sowing seed. Like I said, money answers all things but only God's touch on money can help it to locate you at the right place, the right time, for the right reasons. Only God can touch the hearts of people and cause them to show you favor when you need it most. God made it so that my leave of absence was fully paid with full health coverage. I did not lose one dime. I did not lose any vacation days. As a matter of fact, here's a side note: since I had resigned from the company I was working with prior to my principal training and could no longer use these days for vacation, the company had to compensate me for each day. A year after I returned to work, I received a check for over four thousand dollars! OK, I just *had* to share that.

Now let's go back to my leave of absence. I did not lose my position in the principal-training program. We were still able to tithe and sow seed and we did. I still sang on the praise and worship team at my church. This was part of my sacrifice to my God. When I was feeling better from chemotherapy, I went to class. I completed as many assignments as possible. In May of 2008, I completed my coursework from the principal-training program and from my graduate program. I graduated with a certificate for School-Based Leadership and a second master's degree in Educational Leadership. Hallelujah! It was now summer and I had to find a leadership position for the fall. The school where I had completed my residency decided to hire someone who had been with the school longer and knew the ins and outs of how it operated. So I was disappointed and back to square one. I interviewed with a few schools and found one I really liked. After a few days of negotiation, they offered me a salary that was sixteen thousand dollars more than what I made as a principal resident. Can you say Hallelujah two times? To God be the glory!

Chapter 10
Tithing Testimony #7 Supernatural Debt Cancellation

My husband and I purchased our first home eight months after we got married. We purchased the home in the season when folks were quickly buying homes and then "flipping" them or just reselling them for a way higher price a year later. Well, to make a long story short, we paid too much money for the house we purchased. How much money is too much, you ask? We paid $73,085.15 too much. I know. I know. How in the world did we do that? You live and you learn. When the recent "recession" began, the president in office worked to come up with various programs to help homeowners save their homes. We were in need of such programs. After I pummeled breast cancer by the Blood of the Lamb, I trampled on it some more by defying the odds of remission. God is a Healer and I am grateful that He had mercy on me.

I told the Lord I wanted to have a family and He blessed us with two boys in two years, Sydney and Zachary. The doctors were wrong. The cancer did *not* return. The Bible says that the rain falls on the just and the unjust (Matthew 5:45). My husband lost his job two months before Sydney was born. After he was born, I was eligible for a partially paid maternity leave but after that I would be without income as well. We fell behind in our mortgage because of this. After *years* of paying a hefty mortgage and no longer being able to catch up due to the loss of income and increase in expenses in our household, we applied and were approved for a modification. But there was just one small issue; the loan company was not willing to combine the second loan with the first or to modify it, leaving us with a payment of $616.49 in addition to the new modified amount we were scheduled to pay. We already knew that the loan no longer had value because the value of our home had depreciated and our payments were seriously past due. I called to find out what our options were in terms of loan payoffs and settlements. For the first few weeks, they told us there was nothing that could be done and that we should work to save up money in order to make the necessary payments. Not! What they didn't know is that we knew the loan had already been written off and the value of the loan had depreciated because the value of the house had depreciated. We called again. This time they explained the discount payoff and settlement options and we made a bid for $750, which they did not accept. They mailed a rejection letter to our home and on that letter I wrote, "This debt will be cancelled in Jesus's Name." My husband and I continued to tithe, sow seed, and believe God's promises. We kept our faith level high by replenishing the word of God concerning the seed we had sown. We *needed* God to move on our behalf. We needed this debt to be supernaturally canceled.

We made another offer for $1,500. This offer was also rejected. The representative told us that what we offered was not enough. He said we would need to pay at least $10,000 to $12,000 in order for the loan to be settled in full. We kept speaking God's word and saying scriptures like, "The Lord takes pleasure in the prosperity of His people" (Psalm 35:27), "The heart of the King is in the hand of the Lord" (Proverbs 21:1), and "The Lord shall supply all of our needs according to His riches and glory in Christ Jesus" (Philippians 4:19). We made yet another offer. This time we raised our offer to $2,000. The representative entered it with hesitancy. He said, "This is still too low but I'll try anyway. You need at least $8,000 or $9,000 in order for that department to consider your bid." Well, what'cha know about my God! We received a letter within the next few weeks stating that our bid had been received and accepted. Woohoo! What does that mean? It means that God's favor permitted us to pay $2,000 to fully settle a $73,085.15 debt. We did not have to pay taxes on the canceled debt and it was recorded as "Paid in Full." The debt was gone! Glory to God! That's all folks! It means the blessings of the Lord make us rich and God adds no sorrow with it (Proverbs 3:22). It means that God allowed our tithes, offerings, and

seeds sown to work for us because we were in covenant with Him. We have embraced His dynamic plan
for provision and our lives are better because of it.

Chapter 11
The Acceptable Tithe

What makes a tithe a "good" tithe? How we present our tithe is important. Just think about when you go out to eat at a restaurant. I don't think anybody would look at a poorly dressed server bringing a poorly presented plate of food, laden with strands of hair on a dirty dish, and say, "Oh well, it's the thought that counts!" and begin eating. Especially if you are paying for it. In order to give an acceptable tithe, we should definitely pay attention to some of the details outlined in the word of God. God cares about how we present what we give to Him. The spirit behind the giving is worth more than the amount of money given. Here are a few things to be cognizant of when you are preparing to give your tithes and offerings.

First, it should be set aside and given first. It should be submitted before any other bills or financial responsibilities. It must be the whole tithe; this means 10 percent of your gross income (or net if you plan to pay the balance when you receive your tax refund). Let's take a look at Romans 11:16, which says:

And since Abraham and the other patriarchs were holy, their descendants will also be holy—just as the entire batch of dough is holy because the portion given as an offering is holy. For if the roots of the tree are holy, the branches will be, too. (NLT)

When we give our tithes first, straight off of the top, we give God permission to bless the 90 percent that remains. If the tithe is given appropriately and with the right kind of spirit attached to it, then we can safely say that the rest is blessed! This means that the promises of God are activated and the devourer (the things that cause our money to go as quickly as it came) will not be able to steal away what we've worked so hard to earn and build. Isn't that great?

Secondly, your offering should be included (Malachi 3:8-9). The offering is given in addition to your tithe. There is no specific amount linked to how much money you should give for an offering. It's whatever you give above your tithes. You can give whatever God lays on your heart for an offering, but be sure to give both.

Next, you should consider your tithe as a seed. Don't just give your tithe because it's your duty. You will be shortchanging yourself. Give your tithe because you are honoring God's covenant and remind Him of it. All seeds are predestined to make more of their kind. Think about it; God has placed seed on the earth and He has already assigned purposes to apple seeds, orange seeds, celery seeds, and anything on earth that is able to procreate with or without human assistance. It is our responsibility to give money, which is our seed, an assignment every single time we give. Money takes its direction from us! Link your seed to need. Give your seed an assignment. Tell it what you need it to do. If you have a special prayer request, write it on the envelope. If you need healing or some sort of breakthrough in your family or finances, assign it to your seed. Tell God what your seed is purposed for. Remember, God wants us to "prove him." Try God and watch Him use your seed to bring about a good change in your life.

Our tithe should be cheerfully given. God loves a cheerful giver. If you give grudgingly or angrily, then you should put the money back into your pocket or pocketbook. Pray so that you can get your heart right first and then honor God with your first fruit. Second Corinthians 9:7 says:

So let each one give as he purposes in his heart, not grudgingly or of necessity; for God loves a cheerful giver. And God is able to make all grace abound toward you that you, always having all sufficiency in all things, may have an abundance for every good work.

Let's take a look at how this same scripture (2 Corinthians 9:7) is written in the New Living Translation:

Remember this—a farmer who plants only a few seeds will get a small crop. But the one who plants generously will get a generous crop. You must each decide in your heart how much to give and don't give reluctantly or in response to pressure. For God loves a person who gives cheerfully. **And God will generously provide all you need. Then you will always have everything you need and plenty left over to share with others.**

Isn't this wonderful? God wants to "generously provide all that we need." His idea of provision is for us to have more than enough to meet our needs and still have more than enough to share with others.

Lastly, your tithe should be faith filled. You must believe that God will do as He has promised. If there is any doubt in you, ask the Lord to help your unbelief and He will. Memorize scriptures on God's provision and meditate on them daily. You've got to have an arsenal ready to go when people say and do things contrary to what you believe God will do. I hope this book has clearly shown you why it's important for believers to faithfully give tithes and offerings. Why live from paycheck to paycheck when you can experience harvest-to-harvest, pressed-down, shaken-together, running-over living? Christ died on the cross so that we could have life and have it more abundantly. He wants us to have God's best here on earth and in Heaven. The tithing covenant offers abundance, protection, financial security, productivity, and more. I want to encourage you from the depths of my heart to embrace God's plan for provision through the tithing covenant. Tithe your way out of generational poverty! Tithe your way out of lack! Tithe your way into the career of your dreams! Access the "more" God has by becoming a Believer with Benefits today! "Prove Me now and see if I will not pour you out a blessing you don't have room enough to receive" (Malachi 3:10).

Prayer of Salvation

If you have not received the Lord Jesus Christ as your Personal Lord and Savior, I encourage you to do so today by reciting these words: Lord Jesus, I acknowledge that you are King of Kings and Lord of Lords. I believe you are the Living Son of God. I believe you came to die on the cross for me, that you were buried and rose again on the third day with all power in Your hands. I repent of my old sinful ways. I ask that you will forgive me of my sins and cleanse me from all unrighteousness. I accept you into my heart as the Lord of my life, in Jesus's Name, Amen.

Now, find a loving, Bible-believing, teaching ministry and don't forget to sow into your new ministry and access God's plan for provision by faithfully giving your tithes and offerings.

9 780985 376208